Budavox
Poems (1990-1999)

Todd Swift

Montréal, Québec, Canada

DC New Writers Series edited by Robert Allen
Book design by Andy Brown
Cover photo by Tony Kostadinov

© Todd Swift, 1999

Dépot légal, Bibliothéque nationale du Québec and
the National Library of Canada, 2nd trimester, 1999

Canadian Cataloguing in Publication Data

Swift, Todd, 1966–
    Budavox: poems, 1990–1999

ISBN 0-919688-48-9 (bound)
ISBN 0-919688-46-2 (pbk.)

    I. Title.

PS8587.W5B83 1999   C811'.54   C99-00781-5
PR9199.3.S592B83 1999

DC Books
950 rue Décarie
Box 662
Montréal, Québec
H4L 4V9

DC Books acknowledges the support of the Canada
Council for the Arts for our publishing program.

Acknowledgements

Versions of some of these poems first appeared in *Matrix*, *The Moosehead Anthology*, *Poetry Nation* and in various chapbooks, including *French Maid*, *American Standard* and *Top Twenty*.

I would like to thank certain poets, friends and mentors who helped make this book possible with their close readings, inspiration and support over a number of years: Dr. Ed Lesko, Victor Garaway, Thor Bishopric, Phil Hiebert, Martin Mooney, Peter Forrest, Gordon H. Buchan, Don McGrath, Daniel O'Leary, William Furey, Eric Sigler, Tom Walsh, Dan Mitchell, Steven Heighton, Bob Holman, Adeena Karasick, Nicole Blackman, Steve Luxton, Robert Priest, Phil Norton, Ian Ferrier, Fortner Anderson, Simon Dardick, David McGimpsey, Emily & Bridget Hourican, Derek Mahon, George Szirtes, Zsuzsa Katona, and most significantly for this collection, Robert Allen and Jason Camlot, who made so many important decisions in determining the current selection.

Finally, my family deserves a section of praise to themselves, for encouraging my early "talking paper" habit. Special thanks to: my parents, Margaret and Tom Swift, my grandparents Melita and Ian Hume, Ed Hume, Bev Swift, Jack Swift, Harry Wilson and my brother Jordan.

THE CANADA COUNCIL | LE CONSEIL DES ARTS
FOR THE ARTS | DU CANADA
SINCE 1957 | DEPUIS 1957

Table of Contents

Ars Criminalis	1
A Solemn Meditation on the Fantastic Four	3
Sonnet for the Lobster Diners	5
Kanada Post	6
In the Future	8
Endangered	9
Sara at Domos	10
Budavox	12
Advice Cut Short	14
Curing	15
West of an Idea	16
On Looking into the Modern Poets	18
Albanese Barber Shop	19
Gun Crazy	20
Clear Obscenities	22
Suitor	24
D.O.A.	25
A.D.	26
The Book of Plagues	27
Why I Do Not Carry a Gun	30
Lac Brigden	31
The Road to Rockingham	32
The Lament of Thomas Stearns	33
An Open Letter to Yevtushenko	34
Vuillard's Leopards	35
Paterson Ewen Painting	36
Composition	37
Appreciating Art	38
Morwyn's Story	39
Julian	41
This Was How One Lasted	42
Evening on Putney Avenue	44

The White Kitchen	46
Notes on Helen	47
Waterloo	48
Ten Rose Songs	49
Reds and Oranges	53
Afterward	54
Making Arrangements	57
Trio Facie	58
Honk Your Horn If You Are Paranoid	62
American Standard	64
She Is Asleep	66
Parthenogenesis	67
Rilke from Duino	68
January 20, 1993	69
On a Poet's Blindness	70
Stoker's Valentine	72
Bottles	73
For Pierina at Christmas	74
The Kite Flyer	75
Mary Veronica Swift, 1914-1991	76
Suburbia Mythologica	77
Ways of Counting	80
Florence, South Carolina	81
To Spiders	83
"Flight Delayed"	84
Of Adonis I Sing, and Aphrodite	86
Eros Victorious	88
Aerial Bombardment, Serbia, Spring 1999	90
Gorazde	91

To Sara Egan, my fudgin

Ars Criminalis

Through the head, like a spear,
or a pen in the right eye,
so that the lens stars,
put some language to some good use.
Jab, smithereen and mar,
just make sure the world is not
as it was before.

Too much
has been said of
death, our little sister of gone,
or love, the winking wet cousin
in the car, and all the fingers
that have dawdled in the cake.

I have never met an academic
I could mistake for a gun,
but I have heard the powdering bark
of a pistol in the tongue of a girl
saying her poem.

The wind and the blue-dark
cloth we call the sky never read a book,
and that man, there, is hole-dead,
and the woman, there, bent,
so much over him,
sings more love on her cheek
than all the rain in Singapore.

I need a language that has escaped
from prison and must get far, fast.
So, here in my bare, sudden city
I have no time for trams
and the names they use for saints.
I speak light, carrying hate and hope
something like urgency.

A Solemn Meditation on The Fantastic Four

Gamma Rays pierced them and they returned heroic
though not without difficulties. When all changes
much remains, but different, even unfortunately
strange, and powerful, so that men point in streets,
their hats tumbling off, and women drop groceries,

to see Galactus, or his herald, in bubbles of concrete,
atoms in galaxies in Manhattan, thrown for a challenge.
Earth-shattering conclusions left monthly, balanced
by the sheer crazy threats of barely thwarted annihilation
and what being super frames. *It's clobbering time*, yet

not all matters can be solved with orange-granite fists,
limbs that stretch like gum, a molten body of a boy,
or a girl whose fields are clear as glass but cannot yield
their molecular force. Because human, we love as well
as when, to war, we take our armour on, and fend for Troy

or Helen; each wall that's a breakthrough for one army
is another's black hole, defeat whorling in like vacuum
and nothing left save rubble, weakness and air half fire,
and the rumor of more ruin on the way, the next landing:
the world a place to be conquered by a Silver Surfer, or

Submariner, blowing what belongs to Triton, Hudson
roiling at the emergence of an aquamarine attack, noble
in its grand indifference to the mere lunged New Yorkers,
abashed but inured to wanton villains and their grandiosity
now that the Baxter Building is the Ur-magnet for wild evil.

For, how can Mr. Fantastic knowingly enter the fragile
space of his own beloved, without a shameful thought,
that what simple anatomy has wrought, his husbandry
may undo, with his newfound abilities, pure expansion?
Obscenity is no part of the vows that bind a man to spouse,

but in the broken house that is radiation's special curse,
who can argue for his long-legged will to stay, just so?
And who may know the proper measure of Ben Grimm's
agony: mightier than a slaughterhouse of oxen, still stone
on stone, and tangerine, his hands a clear sign of clumsy

cold, no subtle fingers here, a demolition of thumbs, a face
like a wrecking ball, and all the passion of a normal man?
Might he not want to break down, be regular now, and take
the blind girl in his athlete's arms, again, no pressure to tackle
Victor Von Doom? Consider the Invisible Girl, later Woman,

whose grace is to go unnoticed, who can keep the rain off
with a shrug of atoms, does she want her genius long or short;
maybe after a homely battle, she may turn her back and leave
her powers on, so no marriage can reach, no matter the arms
that struggle to strain and pound at her inviolable places?

For Johnny Storm, no tonnage of car wax or peroxide obscures,
his film idol's grin eats only oxygen and spits lewd fire, his trim
physique a mitochondrion's macrocosm gone supernova. Sure
he's beauty jetting from a flame-thrower, a solar rose, flight
hotly incarnate, a stream of fuel lit and flown across the sky,

lean muscle in a tight blue uniform that accepts the burn...
but this, and less. He cannot lift his playmates to the sun
as he himself may go, but must return too soon
    with lovers to the ground.
They've found, all four, and each as fantastic as
    a bestiary's apocrypha,
a sullen access to the null and void of life, where
    Midas fondled yellow.

Sonnet for the Lobster Diners

Nothing is pretty about a lobster
you can't tear out; the shell's a wreck
of red and claw, someone's idea
of nasty art exploded on the ocean floor;
but the meat is something else,
the sweet soft promise finally come,
when hot butter's delivery slides along
the fingers and the tongue: a story
with an ending twice as happy as the start;
so all the art of eating out the creature
is to take apart the structure like an act
of war, to get to the armistice beneath
the armour: the white tangy peace of flesh
that pulls as it parts with its shellish brother.

Kanada Post

I remember some other life as if it's mine.
Properly, it doesn't belong. I'm far away.
My country is become a stamp and weather,
and what my mother says, on the phone.

And memories — like sausages, suspect,
best not consumed once you think what's
crammed inside. I miss less than I expected.
My old house, too small, the brick dust

and slanting porch, and things, what we
don't mention anymore. The neighbours who
didn't used to be francophone. Another matter.
Hard to talk across a language you don't share.

Unless, at least, you both want to be there.
In the first place. So they moved in, ours
dumped homes they'd spent half lives on,
soon the yards were new others, mowing.

Schools that had been one way, were not, now.
And the snow. It falls and builds great towers,
closing off what is within from what's without.
The blowers with their dark, regurgitated slush.

Trees catch ice and become impressive with April.
My birth month is rain and light like a dancing pair
of skaters. The smell of winter breaking like glass,
and what rushes us, desperate in the air. Running.

The frail blue of early night, in late spring. Shone.
I never loved the ones that went, and not those
that did the replacing. Neither were mine to lose.
It's not a country if it only happens when it's gone.

In the Future

it will be possible
to program sleep
and wake up as any object
so desired: cars,
compacts, microwave
ovens, VCRs, ladies'
razors, laser discs, Ming
vases, plastic gloves,
vibrators, and specially designed
sex-chairs, walking sticks,
lipstick, a former lover.

You will be able to turn into first
one and then another of these things
at will, enjoying the inanimate
splendour of being usable,
reusable, as the case
might be, knowing that
in the next chamber
your friends or mating partner may
already be waiting
as their own favourite instrument
of departure, longing.

Endangered

I was never much good at being observed.
More than altering, I would respond
by going into a subtler spectrum. Astonishing,
the rapidity with which a person pales
out of sight. Out of mind is another thing:

ghosts may get away, they will search you out
when you have responsibilities to answer for,
prayers to pray. Under inspection by a group
of anti-ghosts, they stopped me half-through
the fade routine, at infrared, with a spray

sent finely over the air to find my general form,
looped thin titanium from skull to heel, pleased
well with their delivery. The young, thin scientist,
eager to be cruel, caressed his find, asking
if I needed anything else. I tried bolting,

scrutiny held fast. I could feel my eyes drying
as if they were paints. The technician
in his green coat scratched my iris
for results. He predicted I was
the last of my kind. This meant release.
The electric band glisters at my throat.

Sara at Domos

Something has filled the light
with more than light
was meant for, moving out
the cottage and the tree
but keeping them astonishing,
still and complete, a second
sun or a different set
of colours for a separate eye.

A black dog, vicious and full
tears the sheet of silent air,
not friendly to us being there.
He stalks his gate,
believing he is mythological,
but we know he is local.

This is not the world
we were born to appreciate.
It is elsewhere, thick
with its time and geography,
it has reasons that belong
to its own people.

We came out of the thicket
a mile back, and caught the river
leaving the cathedral,
and the sky less blue than green.
You and I walked quickly down,
your hand my only guide,
with its tinfoil ring.

If we are married, it is here,
natural, unexpected, side-by-side,
suddenly made real
by the depth of what was before.

Budavox

It seemed like a lot of sex at the time,
an opportunity in the offing, with wine,
a succession of blondes, and other names,
girls whose bodies happened to be mine;

and evenings, mornings, always becoming
afternoons, on futons stained with come,
coffee tins overflowing with du Mauriers,
and somewhere a kitchen sink out at sea;

sunglasses and summer dresses tossed
aside, and pierced navels, and green eyes,
and mouths toasting semen and sharp suits
torn at the buttons, and daddy's silk ties;

and down at the elbows, taut ass in the light,
fame buzzing like a bluebottle at the pane,
slapping fiestas of semi-debauchery and full-
blown pain, kisses that lasted long weekends;

boyish bangs and hips sliding out of their plastic
things, and by the stripping candles, nose and ear
rings, glistening, in the background Manchester
bands, and in the cafés, a sense of a wunderkind

entitlement and uneasy living on flimsy pensions,
a sweet maudite auburn moment in the periphery
when she and her lipstick and I in my hubris met,
and all our boulevard fun needed no introduction.

Now the Lycra and the nylon, the flannel and wool
are gone, as are the women who were willing then
to take a bit of else with their something — thin arms
and spoken word — the whole love vision not absurd

as much as blindsided by oncoming maturation,
so that I recall recurring bliss like a 19th century
belief in the world soul, a thing out of era I miss.
No new grief or fashion can revive an outmoded

philosophy, which was what it was, that serial
annunciation of carnal play, driven by anxiety
expectant with lack of confidence and past abuse,
the present a dumping ground for lavish excuses;

where dealers and sly whores, and those who banged
their heads on floors, and punks and junkies, mixed it
up with scores of morose stylish types, hip and sick,
so hell and heaven were cross-dressers renting upstairs,

and coke and opium and assorted cocktails over-spun
the whole wheel of tedium, whose brief consolations
were never dull, but so-ever rare, and when they left,
these demi-friends, they jumped lovers and would tell.

Advice Cut Short

Pray in the least travelled
room in your house,
where her absence is least
likely to appear theological.

Pray with words until,
realizing they were used
several moments in her ear,
they trammel memory,

and are too sad to bear.
Go into the shortest hall
in the shortest month
and lay yourself upon this floor.

The chill of being dead
will move in, next door,
and remind you why we borrow
sugar from sorrow.

Curing

I have discovered a cure for blindness. It involves glass.
You must crush it as if you were churning butter.
Spread the grains upon a kerchief, stolen from a peasant
girl in the fields. Strip naked. This must be done three
weeks before harvest (the moon removed) when the sky
is the colour of veins under an old woman's skirt. Begin
to dance as if dogs were after you. Smear the shards
across your genitals like jam. Whimper like the wind
worrying for the damned. Be careful to bleed against a
wall where recently two lovers have been; gently. Move
away from the spot, appearing ashamed. Bind your
wounds with splinters. Apply broken eggshells lightly to
the open, wandering eyes. In the morning, all is
changed: they will not stray again. When you return the
kerchief, she will thank you, smiling. Look indirectly at
her now. You are in the sun.

West of an Idea

1

Motels are the opposite of fame.
Anyone can enter the same rooms,
turn the television on.
There is always a fat man,
or a skinny man, at the check-in,
and when you sign your name
you do not have to sign your real one;
like a star, in reverse, you can assume
another identity, fall from being known
into the world we disappear into, when
we want to be away from those who know us.
Here, it is possible to be someone we once
imagined becoming, or worse, much worse.

2

Motel strips dot the highways, easy
as filling stations, and the register's page
always turns. Nothing surprises:
cigarette burns on the carpet, toilets
that flow at their own pace and time,
blinds that shut, and a small refrigerator
for beer or caviar. And twin beds, for two
or more occupants. And a closet, with bare
hangers, waiting for coats to be put on them.
The Bible, of course, and four glasses, enclosed
in wax paper, and a phone, sometimes
without a dial. You go direct to the man
at the front desk, who can connect you
to the rest of the world. When you stay

for days, they will never enter and change
your sheets, if you leave the sign that says:
Do Not Disturb. They respect your right
to privacy — you've paid for it, you get it.

    3

And so it is that when the party is thrown,
the bottle taken out of the bag, the joints
rolled, the needle introduced, the films shown,
the sex had, it all takes place in total secrecy.
This is not your TV studio, any more.
No director watches from a close distance,
no one says: that's a wrap, that's all for today.
Whatever happens, goes on. Until it is over.
When it is over, you are dead. Someone
you brought in to your home-away-from-home
has gotten out of hand. And now they come
straight in, break through, cameras flashing,
the boys from the station, exposing exactly
what you intended to keep hidden. A
simple desire to do things, differently, that is all.
And, in your realm of seedy departure,
you did the rough and strange life a favour,
you gave it a queer allure it never had before.

On Looking into the Modern Poets

I have wanted to be in your period
dress that looks like it smells of
chalk, roses, and secondary wars,

all your gin halls and yellow letters,
your stiff words and overseas betters,
your gassed deaths, your tight fears,

the way even your bodies took
sleep, shaped in old modern beds.
On your faces you wear

wire-rimmed age and glasses
and retro hair cuts, showing off
your dated, quite angular skulls

like trench soldiers in historic plates.
You appear to know nostalgia's arc,
look gentle doing other things

besides what's important, writing:
out a window, carefully smoking
squinting to the sun, off-camera.

Albanese Barber Shop

I enjoy the part
where the barber
lathers the nape
of your neck,
and it's warm,
like entering a woman,

but on the outside here,
and soap is sliced
from its slide
down your throat
to the collar, the blade
loose in his expert fingers,

quickly by the ears,
tracing exactly the outline
of blood he doesn't let flow.
I love the answer
the barber has for long hair:
end it, keep lines short.

He cuts a fine poem
in his shop. I figure
he could kill me
for my money
if he did not love
my business so.

Gun Crazy

Against the world, just us.
Behind, a trail of gas stations,
green grocers, meat-packing plants,
banks, knocked over. Telexes

clatter like town gossips across
America: *Bart Tare and Laurie Starr,
armed and dangerous.* In your quick eye
I feel most wanted. How did it all begin?

Was it that I needed a nightmare to fall
asleep in, my sweet? Neon wakes me,
I peel back blinds to jackhammer rain,
shake a Lucky from the pack, and light.

Behind, on the tangled bed, you are mine,
every inch of your easy hunger, your fear
cold and material in the night. Murmuring
like a baby, baby you are so alive, I so dead

in this mixed-up journey. Where are we two
going? When we get there, how will we know
we've finally arrived? Mexico, possibly,
but the bills are marked and the Feds hot

on our tails. The first time we met, I shot
five matches off the crown on your head
at a carnival, won five hundred bucks.
The moment the matches flared, I knew

my bullets would always be true, direct.
You kill out of a necessity verging on need,
I cannot squint the eye down to that degree,
my hand trembles at the sight of flesh targets.

Still, I'll end up putting a bullet in your heart
somewhere up in the mountains, in the mist.
That first night I aimed and squeezed
I should not have missed. You wake and call

me over to the bed. Then I'm down in your arms
and kissed. Your mouth sets off all four alarms.
How can a man be so made from moments
of early loss? I was always gun crazy, so good

at one clear thing, hitting what I could barely see.
I see nothing in the darkness now, only
one part moving on the bed, my body
pressed like a pistol into the small of your cries.

Soon, at Madera National Park, us starved cougars,
they will circle in, and there will be one last release.
Laurie, we took lives just to live high, so
we deserve to die up here like this, I guess.

Clear Obscenities

It happens somewhere,
in a room filled with natural light
coming through picture windows

beyond which are round hills, swimming
pools, and semi-tropical vegetation.
It must be California.

The furnishings are spare,
ultra-modern, hip, designed:
black leather and chrome,

spaced unevenly, far apart
on the gleaming marble floors.
She kneels and extends her hands.

Her arms are sheathed
in black plastic. Here eyes are covered
by Ray-Bans. Her head is tight

in a rubber hood, which emphasises
her mouth, and her long jaw.
She has bright red lipstick on.

His hands hold her smooth head,
guiding her forward. She wears a collar.
Perhaps she exists only for this.

The furniture in the room is still.
He moves forward, her face retreats,
an expression of total concentration

mixed with slack reverence and blank hope,
as she waits for the idea of a reward,
in exhortation, in the begging position.

The man obliges, coming as she bends
her head, down to her cupped black bowl,
seeming intent, wholly present, nearly fed.

Suitor

Brushing your eye
it came out.
Embarrassed, I bent quickly
to retrieve your blue object
under the skirts of the end table.

When I brought it up
to your dark place,
I found you had forgotten
you had ever seen from it,
moved your head aside, gently
to indicate disinterest
as you do when you are tired
of my brushing of your hair.

Understanding very little but my duty
I went at the other,
in a moment had you
in completed darkness.
Your head raised itself, backward, quietly,
prepared to not remember, ever,
what would be next.

D.O.A.

— dedicated to Vincent Lang, d. Memorial Day, 1996

I would like to report a love affair
that is very over. My own.
Her luminous poison is all through my system,
I've been running through busy streets like doom,
my silk tie flying over my shoulder,
knocking the fedoras off completely strange men,
not noticing the runs up the legs of secretaries,
skewed hems, refusing to pay anyone
for rides on the trolley cars, going up and down.
My heart has the limited life span
of a mayfly. It's due to explode any time now,
and when it does I will immediately die.
The Grim Reaper's got me on a very short leash,
so short it feels I've been unleashed by him.
I have twenty-four hours, maybe a week
to find the guy who did this to me
and settle my accounts. I want information.
Give it to me straight, Doc. Every second counts.
Talk! Could anything toxic in my bloodstream
have come from something as nice and red
as my gal's lipstick? There's gotta be
a better explanation. Her kiss is her alibi.
Sure, that's it. Fate's had it in for me, ever since
I got here, already lonely and walking dead.

A.D.

For several minutes all we do
is undress, biting. There may be light,
but one black shoe breaks the bulb off,
the other shuts the door. Music

does not outdo our louder music: your
name, mine, over and over
the bed. We are tumbling. There
may be others, elsewhere. Therapy,

memories, what our children will appear
like, all this speculates in the hall,
we are inside another room. Nature
adores us, we involve vacuum

in the act of sucking. Turns
take time through a share
of each twitch, each organ, twined
in roman numerals, reversed.

Well versed in the fall beyond sex, we slip
on the other's skin, untaxed, vegetable
matter, a multiple absence replete
with our rehearsal of the next life, carnate.

The Book of Plagues

There, in your face, is the face I would touch,
though the hands I carry are too long.
They would starve you, my hands,
like long iron poles set in the ground
for a prison, and all the birds strutting beyond,
for the guards lay the bread there, taunting.
No one has thought to publish the reasons
for the severity of the sentence, the crime done.

My hands would make a church of a rain barrel.
How the water is scooped slick off the portion
uppermost to the sky, reflecting a fluid altar
black with autumnal wafers I call fallen leaves.
There is, upon your face, the idea of a church
built on water, a less modern notion.
The effects of motion I strike with my hand
upon the flat of the rain water in the barrel,
move the light there, forcing a second face,
a persistent change of emotions on it,
a looking-away glass.

Alas, I have forbidden
food to enter my church. It stands empty
of nutrition, my very tall cathedral
of poured rain, curved in the wooden barrel,
left out to contain the elements that tremble
persistently, from out of the sky, fallen.
Your face needs light as it does bread
but in this climate skin grows sick on the sun.
So gather a white mask of protection
and spread your tan fingers across your face,

obscuring your red mouth. Spread
the white solution of protecting oil upon
your lips, like semen smearing a rose.

I will not resolve to stop at kissing your red
mouth only. I will spend the better part of Easter,
all Lent, taking your clitoris upon my tongue.
I am that young. I love the positions
of the light, in the church made of stone
water-boiled to columns of reflected cloudshadow.

Your face is a gradual tenderness of failing.
I touch your hair and it is made of rain. This
is desire turning to beauty. This is the gesture
of the proverbial madman, ruining his clothes
in the open square, moaning far past
the clocktowers, wailing higher than the pitched
moon, its pew of stones pale and empty, now
that the prayers in the sky are over, children
gone that once bent forward with tiny hands
and signalled to their parents, and the churchgoers,
that they held a small belief, enough to grow it, up
through the palms they leaned together
out over the boneroof of the night, as the rain makes
pillars out of air.

I wish to visit your mouth with sorrow's shape.
Never is there enough skin to stretch over
the both of us. We remain somehow, absolute,
absolutely identical to our own place. If
we were removed from our pockets
of space, we would not become the other.
I cannot lean far enough into you
with my hands, to believe the prayer.
There is a religion between us which is
an absent region of despair.

Be strong and break the water, the church will hold,
it is the ones who have run out the far door, who are
terrified of the lions roaring in at the main gates.
Your beauty is a transforming of desire, I have printed
out the Bibles myself, each is bound in black marble
and ripples with the undue presence of light reflected
through water, which is produced from an eye.
The eye is a tiny ocean stirred through a lens, uncorrected
by the Lord. And on the first day of my eyes
I opened upon angels shaped like lions, who roared the air
like meat was soon to be unrolled from the beasts, like bark
from a medicinal tree.

Remember that each person who has lived
or is living is more full of things
that have happened, or are due to occur,
than any book that is ever to be written.
We will die sufficiently ourselves
to never require opening past the earliest chapters
until resurrection shall close the tome
and we no longer see mere words. The body risen
twice is what language should aspire to fear.
The language of bread and water is the voice
of the open air prison released from you
and come to me. Turn your face
to my face, and join tongues, long hands.

Why I Do Not Carry a Gun

It fits perfectly
into a mouth.

It contains bullets.

It is the colour
of dark leather.

It is the length
of a cock.

Because, crouching
on one leg, it can
eliminate a room
of persons. Immediately.

It can be easily concealed.

Because it feels good
in the hand.

Because I would stroke
your cheek gently
with it, often.

Because I want to.

Lac Brigden

The lake is black with the green. Writing
a lake is to add a shade. Four hundred
trees are apparitions, leaning into
the space, which ruffles. Beating beneath
this is whatever you choose to haul upwards,
unleash among the flies, the hovering sun

patterns, the sculptures of drowned clouds,
pushing explosion into quiet covering. A poem
drifts its isolated green raft on oil drums
pumped full to bursting with air, linking
the rusted ring by the ladder to the Ajax bottles,
dropped by cement to the sludge fifteen feet below

the edge of where a sky gets wet and dark.
Two girls from an adjacent cottage soon haul
themselves onto this mobile patio, sun their shape
together into earthy unison and heat. A lesson
palpitates, of going over sand, and arriving
at a shivering looseness, barren but for fire.

The Road to Rockingham

I passed the lab boys
with their busy vials
and the kid selling maps
to Fatty Arbuckle's

hopped the fence,
opened my wrist
and shouted: here's your evidence,
here it is!

The Lament of Thomas Stearns

I caught a fly this morning
taking its constitutional
across my bare wrist, domed
it under a teacup.
The perfect china shook.
I went upstairs to shave.
The razor held a special status
in my thoughts, bare bodkin
in the bath water. Downstairs
again exactly an hour later
by the cuckoo clock, still
a wild penitent insisted on outlet.
No air soon would give it notice,
the table setting calmed.

All my life I have wanted
to take my fist down,
right onto glass. Begin
a violent process, send birds
scuttling off the near branch.
That would be an event.
Like all the island curled under ash,
bodies with no motion, burnt dolls
in a crusted house, the lava flat
and sullen now that the fire's done,
cold as a widow's night-cap.
Instead, I created a second life
for the creature, tilted an inch
of rim to aperture flight.

An Open Letter to Yevtushenko

That is like us, to go on thinking
things remain, simply, but rain dries
after it is freshly fallen, and the air
darkens constantly at the night;
and however it is described,
the planet we must consider our own
will engage the moon and sun
somehow in difference, each season's quarter.

Our lives move along still more unevenly:
without recovery, discovering a complex removal
of acts, decisions, persons we have known.
You've heard all this before, I know, but
this is to show I am still young enough
to attempt wisdom for an occupation
in poems filled with murder as well as berry-picking.

After all, were you really the angry nihilist Zhenya,
who flooded their huge stadiums with teenage fans
hungry for readings active with football and Stalin?
How is it your tears dried so suddenly on the skin —
at the realisation no one was necessarily watching now
your relief — his body passing like Lincoln's
in the hearse a nation died to gather around?

Vuillard's Leopards

Remember those paintings by Vuillard,
the ones spotted yellow and brown
in the background like a leopard?
That was wallpaper, my favourite scene.

If legal, I could stroll
right up and take them down
to my room, to have at times
to touch heightened softness, creviced silk

able to unravel like petals and become screens
a white geisha might come out from silently,
a woman whose materials have forgotten how to rustle
in motion made across, and through, rooms.

Paterson Ewen Painting

Welding to the board,
one hand at the ruined head,
a corrugated bolt of fiery tin
to chain the wall, landscaping
in the quiet storm emanating beyond

bludgeons the scene with steel, grease,
colours killed to pour, and done,
nothing lasts but the trembling sheet,
effects of darkness paling at the edge
to mountains sawed in with teeth.

Composition

The room I am in while I write this
is a large room filled with light from
the place she stepped out of. Filled

with traces of smoking, taken-off clothing,
the abandoned furniture of desire. The room
I am in contains no less than five chairs,

and no more than one person. I am
drowning in my own bath: the ending quiet
is so familiar, death might be my bowels

moving. Everything is halfway in its place,
the scatter-guns of August blew into Autumn.
Now September empties the trees, a dark bladder

is bright red.

Appreciating Art

Let me strangle the curator
and amble over to you
at last, brushing off the plaster
cast, whitening, like a coat of flour,
your resembling breast, which bears
so much, like the rest of you,
a disturbing likeness to yourself.

Your mouth is perfume (flower red)
and moisture shaken from it
bumbles ripe motion
in its fluid, fertile tread,
worrying description, like living
tropics groping light
within an English, bounded garden.

Phantasmal limb; de Milo's shadow;
Eastern wisdom; talking peepshow;
transparency on an overhead
charting the relative decline of business
in the rainy months; all these your kiss
is, at once, no longer elusively draped
in puce velour, raised chest high from the floor:
dour, dry and nakedly fiction.

I have come to appreciation late
in my career. Your skin is just
as you told me it would be, as
I blushed to touch, and instead
settled on relentlessly observing
its eternal accounting, booked in marble.
I marvel at its waves: pure synthesis of energy, milk and blood.

Morwyn's Story

I ate my horse.
I am the Yellow Dwarf.
I ride my Spanish cat
and brandish a toothpick

sword. In all the tales
I have read you
from the Blue and Green Books
as you tried to fall asleep

in the middle of an enchantment
or murderous spell, or axe
ready for the ripe children,
as I made up caresses

in your hair, and you
snuggled, safely away
from childhood, the wicked
cripples and aquiline queens,

I used the voice you loved
when I said
your favourite grotesque line:
I ate my horse.

Ate it because I eat beauty,
and spit the elegant bones;
came riding to court you
hunched and dark

in my tiny rags,
thick claws fatted
with bulbous rings
swiped from svelte gypsies;

having picked the wrong white
cortège clean; the steed
skeletons belonged to
the true prince: more immaculate,

but I have one other, magic, thing
besides my unsuitable profession
suspended by broken words alone
and corned with walking bareshod:

I bring my real hand over
to wake you for the ending,
yawning myself, but steadfast
for telling, utter

the infamous diet
of unfit ogres:
I ate my horse, again. Then turn
from your sleeping and dream of worse.

Julian

Julian has a hat that is passed down
from his father and it is indestructible.

He lent it to me for the duration of his visit,
four nights and three days,

and I wore it constantly, pretending
to be him. His instructions were simple

in the extreme: not to care for it,
not to protect it from the elements,

for the way of caution leads to weakness,
and the wearer would ruin the quality of the worn.

Instead, he urged me to carry it in to the shower
in the mornings, and crumple it

strongly in the hand, throwing it across the room
with disdain. It lasted my attempts

to destroy its casual form, its legitimate brim.
He left promising he would send me one of my own

in about eight to ten weeks. It never came.
I intend to carry my bare head around in similar fashion.

This Was How One Lasted

I used to pretend I was a dolphin
when I swam in the lake.
I was a boy then, my skin smooth
and untanned, because I read
all day on the lawn, my legs
covered by a blue towel, with a pine
tree marking my chair and book
in a high, clean shade, the light
tart needles of windblown air.
Twice in a day, only, would I
become upright, and go down
to the water, once before noon
and then again near evening.
I was thin and young, with shivers
and would wait for something
to call me in. Often I heard no reason
to dive for an hour, staying there
watching the sunbathing girls
on the raft, turning slowly
along the chain that tied them
to the bottom, the gallon cans
filled with sand. Spiders, landed
like aliens on the moon of green
linoleum of that raft, made it their
ghastly headquarters, so I never
went there. Finally, I would walk in
until the line of my belly
was drawn in the lake, risen
over my startled penis, and I would join
the line, and descend. I had no water eyes,

closed and forced a form I was to plummet
straight free. This was my extending moment,
all union and calm, the sweep and underneath
of sensation, all motion caused to rhythm
and tense, untensed flight in the springs
that crossed my body, heat and cold turned on
and off, like faucets, as I passed, a fast and silent
submarine. Unborn and beyond exposed things,
saved in the water, I began with nothing
but hands and a lidded mind, and life
and thought through to the ocean where I was elsewhere,
also, at the same time, my bones a sweetbread, slid
into the mammalian sea, a knife. I never came up
on behalf of oxygen, searched for pockets where
I stayed, my feeling was this was how one lasted
after drowning and dead, was better than above.

Evening on Putney Avenue

When all the lawns are shutting off,
neighbours each with a porch light to close,
I stand in my driveway and smoke alone
not allowed to smoke inside my house
and look down Putney Avenue, left and right,
as I was taught to do before crossing,
but stay in my place, watching for the moon
to change, as people wait for green.
The boy and the girl shoot past in a red car,
she turns her face, an instantaneous affair,
then it takes Mortlake. A family with another

girl slowly talks through the leaves,
acknowledging no part of me. I step back
into the lilacs, to let them go without
having to recognise my slight presence.
She also turns, her eyes see my new haircut,
but she goes on with her parents,
her skinny legs in black summer shorts.
She accompanies my mind to the end of the block.
Come back, come back and love me,
I almost say. Once, this was the street where
I played soccer-baseball, and kick-the-can.

I must know the ground here like no one else,
the way the caterpillars crawl along the arm.
I am middle into my third decade now, at home
to have what comes back after a breakdown.
I lost a lot here, and then I was gone.
I toss the cigarette off the curb and prepare

to go back in. My parents are in there, warm.
The spring air is chillier than you might expect.
For all the things I do not have, I have
this night, suburban and sublunar, to collect,
like a paperboy cast in stone.

The White Kitchen

Yes, you are gone
and I believe that bodies rot
when buried in the ground,
though as to what happens
to living creatures
that walk their peripheries

in a distant town, assuming
the invisibility of mere departure,
I am helpless to say.
Your hair is likely now
to be dirty blonde
(as always), your height

still vertical, to my chin, if
my head were present to compare.
Not dead then, but distant.
On the occult telephone
your voice sounds
as oddly rushed as from the ether,

summoned by a crone.
I can add nothing new
to metaphysical conjecture,
I am no oiled and bound Egyptian,
have no name for what's been done
here in your absence's white kitchen.

Notes on Helen

All that is not dust
is still dust
under her body.

Vanity is a brass bird
weighing shuffling paper down.
The wind ruffles the stained colours.

The world is not in her.
She has only one body.
She is the eye's swivel.

The farthest truth
is beneath her skin.
To kiss is to know nothing.

No present can be offered
she does not despise.
Heaven loiters in her thighs.

Men without teeth
grind their hands
into powder for her youth.

Her imprint on the bed
leaves a grave.
Her body is never lightly given.

All that is dead
is in her.
The rest look on.

Waterloo

The nature of distance often eludes me.
After our meeting, you remain
no matter what the weather.

Touch could be the addition of departure.
Of all possessions, yours is least at my command.
Regardless, I strongly maintain this lie:

if not for the air's consistency I could reach
through and produce the city, the bed, you live in.
I walk outdoors with just such a suspicion.

Around the next corner the dimension is waiting, torn,
possible worlds seeping out, like a bathtub overflowing
down through the kitchen ceiling.

Ten Rose Songs

1

I send you
a thousand roses,
too many
for you to hold,
because each of them
is love,
is a year,
is anything
a house is too big for.

2

On my teller's salary
I will be able
to afford roses
at three per day
from now on,
barring failure
of the bank,
if I do not eat
very often.

3

I like the thought:
you having to find places
to put a thousand roses
(more than that boy sent,
than any boy will send)
thinking how perfectly
ridiculous they all are.

4

Poetry is a flood,
but since I am not a poet
and wanted something
startling and difficult
to handle, I send you
a rose times one thousand,
an act
financially overzealous.

5

I am glad I startled you.
A thousand roses is my way
of saying each of them
again and again
is the moment
I kissed
your body
and kept on for hours.

6

Don't ever go.
Ten thousand other roses
are on their way.
I've broken
my account,
will soon be
deep in debtors' prison.
I want you to laugh
at the vans that can never,
with all the orders, stop
bringing such wondrous
red explosions
to your door.

7

Start building a rose-house
to keep your countless roses!
They are minutes and seconds,
their arrival tells time,
it is the moment
I first saw you,
over and over again,
for me to dream of,
as I languish
in this stone hole.

8

Obsessed?
I was only a clerk,
not like a madman
or a druggist, but
I feel love like any artisan,
my red suspenders removed
in case I hang, but
who could die knowing
you are being murdered
by an avalanche of roses?
Certainly not me!

9

I am sending you
twenty-one roses,
one for every year
you have been born,
and I am sorry
I am not there
to see if you are happy.
All I can do is wish you well

at the restaurant you work at.
I guess the roses resemble
your childhood, the knees
you scraped before I got a chance
to make it better.

        10

I am sorry,
they were all out of roses,
so I am sending this instead.
Put the paper in a vase
filled with lukewarm water
from your tap.
It will flower,
language is plentiful
where I come from.

Reds and Oranges

How does blood get in?
I ask her, preparing
a tray of them, stained
and magnificently bleeding
despite my ignorance of the means
by which she made them this way.

Putting one in my mouth, her finger
rests inside, to catch a nectar
special to this season, and I rely
on a difficult sensation, pleasing
to everything I own, to answer
the body of my question.

Enough to say, *it does.*

Afterward

I have been careful with the axe.

I have put everything away.

I have been, for several years,
everything promised you.

Seldom has it seen so much darkness,
this night, gathering
itself, as if for an announcement
of greater weather.

The snow in the yard is heavy.
It is capable of covering
the ground.

I have left nothing out
that could be stolen. I ran into
the blizzard, with both arms
lifting what you wanted,
brought in. I am tired now
and want you to touch me.

I lied for several years to you,
Raina. I did this
out of love, with conviction
softly on my brow.

What have I done with the gloves?
Raina, darling, I told you
that on purpose they have been left
to gather for an entire winter

the waste of frost,
to crack.
Relentless, the amounts possible,
that gather.
Four poems I refused you
my love, four never given.

The fifth lies at the foot of the garden,
and is waiting,
with eyes closed, without speculation.

I was once a child, yes,
why do you ask? Raina,
you were also. Do you not understand
how terrible it is to find distance
at the heart of coming closer?

I have put everything where it belongs.
The pages are away, the desk
is neat, as if it had never been committed
here. The house will be closed
for summer. All here will be closed.

There is no Raina. I carry the axe
backwards, to its handle,
and retire
to the cellar,
where dark, swollen vegetables keep quiet. Always.

This morning you woke up earlier
than me, and stole
to the attic, where I am preparing
the anthology, and tore out
that poet you tell me is awful.
I know he is.
I am not ready to ask you

to give his poems back.
Keep them.

Raina is five-foot-seven.

I have no photographs
of either of us, separate
or together. I remember
through the sensation
of touching cold windows
and recalling
that each event is
itself, preparing
no other.

Each event recalls its own coming.

I have left nothing out for the night, Raina.

Making Arrangements

I will not go to my father's Russian funeral,
she said. The Soviet Army Chorus
sang in the darkness, red Hungarian wine
more dusk than dawn in her glass.
All the way to her Orthodox grandfather's
burial in the limousine, the mute monk
sat stroking his long beard while
she ignored his advances, in the back.
If the purpose of such ceremony is to observe
one's own passing, pleased with the care family takes
to memorise another death, pass good riddance on
to the ground, then why use a language
the spirits and the living equally forget? she asked
me. Perhaps the situation of leaving this table
where we talk is inconceivable without
incomprehensible symbols, I answered, pouring myself
more red from the clearing bottle. Candles cancelled us,
and replayed in the corners, under the windows,
across the posters, on the walls. Her husband
had been quietly watching our conversation, gathering
how closely I kept my eye upon the circular pieces
of her spectacles, reflections happening there, the slight
curve of her right nostril, the smallest detail
which excites passion. When you die, Mishka,
he said, I will see to it you are burned
and scattered instead.

Trio Facie

1 Convex Rex

At tissue limit, porous verge,
time Constantinople's light,
speeds return. Membrane break,
the Dutch wreck, diverse pains
to take the curved realm

and flower the palm to the floor;
where Jesu barks, Adam singes
the eventide. Eisenstein's mons
stages rocketry and lands Rhine,
the head cell's Lloyding it over

alloying London — Ah clocks —
roll the back and façade out
and over; Bethlehem's steel
coiling at the horizontal frisk.
Franca, Francesca, Liszt, Lingua,

Latinate, potentate, Franz, Apollo,
Paolo, fall, Dido, engulf, Donne.
List the open until it swells,
no brain can contain the *raison
d'Artagnan*, or appellate, courting

the foster adventures of concupiscence,
which is thriving everything.
The scope, range and wrack of Spain
means *rien* in rotten German, say
history is a grain of Beethoven,

and the Ninth is the *n*th degree
of separation from the Second return,
cruising the crushed Vienna of space,
where Sissi reins in her running stallion
on the roiling track of eternal ebullience;

we all love a good ending. To begin
is worst, and yet did tell. What matters
is somewhere, find that. Meanwhile
envelope slide, event melt and flood.
God is Grenoble, and if so, then.

2 Origin Regina

Love happens to not alter
moon, Saturn or sun house,
deter the goat-footed ocean,
perturb serene Euclid's work.
Nor did it charm the mover

of this, our entire set of sets.
Not orb, web, wave, cylinder,
no kind of iron, silver, gold,
wheel or shudder has been
made by the great emotion.

Of everything, very little has it
touched. But what has known
the full pulse, spun then farther
than father, star or green, thrown
rubbing walls with frictions there,

where sub-set and substance mark
the broken halter of existing forms,
and the mother horse, nothingness'
rides being like an unbridled whore.
Out even more still, felt and owned,

I crown love now the supernal utility
in a wilderness with all power gone.
Fierce light needing no source to burn
itself upon common oil night, it shone
so before child/heaven and the barn.

3 Pince Prince, Pense Nez

Inez at Penzance, did the sea swallow
or was the salt your tongue's doing,
supreme *voleur de valeur*? Penance
did piracy on your highs,
your lows were dogs themselves,
flinging their slick skins
on the mackerel and the men,
your oiled thighs enough deck
to swab any conscience clean,
even a Dane's. That morning,
an English accent in the spray,
did you see the ocean station
itself about seven leagues away,

undulating eyesore of bracken,
broken-spavined spire of Poseidon,
shocked blacks and fuming greens,
or were you the hideously seen one?
Inez, does a penile or a vaginal force
fire your imagination more,
walker of the cobblestones, where
the very model of a major verse
veers from better to far worse
while lyric poets from the previous
century dive in and drown, as roses
of their own creation, cast like odes
on the humped trampoline of the waters?

Odious matters and poor manners
may intrude on your dismal sojourn
so early in the dawn, *dame sans clue*,
but why then do you query the brine,
if salmon and crab cannot Quine
the illogic of the sentenced lines
hanging themselves out to dampen
in the cold, cool undulations at the quay?
Inez, dream women and vexed *femme*
whose quim is demi-legendary to me,
does your willing finger enter your pussy,
or does my imagination make that happen
only, my manual dexterity mere temerity

in this temporal leap to rapine interrogation?
Why so much suspicion today, Miss, since
this is what the field is open to, nay demands,
though the sands in your sandals quicken
your quick pace away, toward the bench,
where, dear nameless wench, Inez, you bend
to undo your stockings and reveal your thighs;
and in the doing of that nonsense show us
meanly how vicious is the urge to miss none
of the positions of a beauty's dish, unscooping
in the generous light of a seaside resort's vacation,
while the bleary inlet slides and grinds its thing,
and you, who are supremest here, come to nothing.

Honk Your Horn
If You Are Paranoid

I am becoming afraid of everything.
This is not a good situation.
Everything is what supports the world.
But suppose it should let go?
I am. Holding everything in perspective
is a tiring spectator sport, the reality

is that when you begin to lose it, big time,
you are already there, lost. Back
is a long way forward, something like
eating a bowl of spiders to overcome
a fear of webs. Not very pleasant,
frankly. Once, my principal came back

from Africa when I was ten, with some
chocolate-covered locusts, and offered them
to my class, sitting on the floor like little Indians;
we ate them, but not me. I was too suspicious then,
as I am now, of such weird delicacies from men.
The world involves a series of plane crashes,

and beautiful women taller than myself. One
of them is my girlfriend. Suppose she was
to offer herself to me, all covered in locusts,
would I eat her sweet tasty bits, or run for cover?
When you turn off a light at night, who says

it will come on in the morning? Not General
Electric. Not even such a gifted multinational
can promise us such permanent illumination.
They know, the suits in their great towers, the world

is all about uncertainty, of that they are certain;
the stock market plunges and spumes free like a dolphin
on that safe basis. There is safety in numbers. Not

all of us will die in the next fiery Boeing lunge
in Chicago or Bombay. Some of us will stay up
to catch the report, shaking our heads before going
to bed, turning out the hall light on the way, musing
that could have been me flying to Jakarta, if only
I had an oil refinery there, that might have been me.

Usually, we slip in baths or fall down weak-limbed ladders,
or stick pulsing, fluid fingers into the wrong sockets,
on-the-job victims of tables and lists, the certainty
that something is coming loose somewhere in the multitudes,
somewhere a boy is loading his AK-47, precisely
to kill your family, your loved ones, everything you see.

American Standard

The Turbine
Rosenheim
is a Berlin
night-club on Eisenhowerstrasse

set in a bunker, housing
ground zero on the floor:
the sound system
closes around the cement walls

pouring confinement, pounding;
the German bodies never cease
trying to get through
power, noise.

The impulse to dance
is enough to regain
forgiveness. Her lenses
present perfect mirrors, her lips

are bright as cherry-red Chevrolets,
bubblegum traded once
near the U.S. army base; her
dress a series of hems talked back

to serious cuts and limitations.
The orange gas
spreads. The violence style
is their only

best defence. It is inviolable.
The doors open at midnight,
curtains drawn to keep the tourist out;
for one hour at dawn, the most devoted

dancers, having stayed, must wait
on the scooter-mad curbs, on fenders,
for the municipal by-law, forbidding music
between the hours of five and six:

some Minister of Importance
has a bedroom nearby.
Some drink Coors and come back
for the end, then drive direct

to secretarial school, work, by nine.
Crew-cuts, Beastie Boys T-shirts,
bomber jackets, and sideburns
on all the boys. The war was won,

after all, by American men.
The wall is so close it could be
the next night of fun,
a dirty little membrane.

(Berlin 1987)

She Is Asleep

This pulse and heap is all of it.
Against your sleep, I stifle
an awe as crimped, as plain,
as wooden Death, wherein
corpsed, convict ash resides
on flames, humanoid, like any
roadside agony, the crushed bush

of blood that was some beast's
answer to light. Angelic impudence
quivers in the blue corners
where dark flaps, constant with
my heart: a soft interrupted action,
black and many as pumped shot.
Then, sweatered in white knots

of wool, every ounce of holiness
there is pours onto you, every inch
of the stars Alighieri jammed Love
through, sets themselves on stun.
Impulsed by such a surround, I
finalise anew, incensed what passes
for forever shivers when she moves.

Parthenogenesis

The light in the morning you left me
went through red in the glass.
Nothing so trite as lasts. But this

is where I will not part ways with love.
If I recall how you have spoken
as you slept, the sight of tampons

in the cupboard, scattered clothes
you would not put back, your head
with its three bumps, finally removed

by the surgeon, the new way I handled your skull
as I thought only of our inextinguishable
need: then I am never to be without.

What hair is shaved, what fluid spilled,
is the correction of anatomy's guilt,
but there are books enough in here for that.

That we held half, that half lingered,
in mutilated silent pause before our former
loss, and kissed with the curiosity that opens

bandages, left us, at morning, numb as ends,
but attempting return, stumbling straight
like the first sun after the second night.

Rilke from Duino

Princess, I compose out of anything you send me,
enveloped by the prowess of the unrelenting angels
I summon to address your elegies. Castles unnerve

my childlike bearing, I hear voices out of order,
uncommon ones that clamour for outlet, when
I have no provisions for their hunger, except

setting pen to paper, as I do now, in a frenzy
of exceptional purpose, mixed to plunge further
past them or to entertain such wanton visitors.

I stay all hours by the light, praying for an end
to this insistence of delight. Were it possible
to praise by day, but then is the one chance I

own to rest. Eternity must lie in wait for this
work's finishing, when I am done holding outer
references. Already I am bent on dream proportions,

thought of our epistolary conversations sends a heat
upon my forehead that mere hands cannot minister
away. Thus is love this ready to enter and employ.

January 20, 1993

What an unbelievably sad day.
I have just watched the woman I love
fly away in a plane. Meanwhile
Bill Clinton is getting his hand raised.

He'll be President of the United States
by the time she lands in Seattle.
The airport, after she went through
the frosted doors to get her bags X-rayed

is like an empty zoo. Space for all sorts
of absent animals. I have three miles
of corridor to myself, push invisible
baggage about. Since she passed beyond

the frost of those doors I've been a porter
with no one to carry nothing for.
You could say: that man is lost.
In the lounge I raise a Bud to the stars.

On a Poet's Blindness

She informs me in her spacious loft
There is no God, only a writer's craft.

I ask her if such a thing as love
Could live through the heart's sieve.

She laughs and shows me her new skin
Where the ink entered and it was broken.

She is marked with images that last,
A woman without history, but a past.

She tells me it's time to fuck,
Wide to open and deconstruct.

It is a needful act to perform
And later the body is still warm.

Though as for her soul that isn't there,
It chills the blankly falling air.

Extremes of cold and heat are flat
When the senses do not penetrate.

There were saints who saw a light
And held a small, sharp chain tight.

There was once a point so great
It might have put a halt to hate.

There have been lovers, true,
Who touched as if they knew

The highest art is to touch with care
And raise up the bright ascending air.

Stoker's Valentine

The throat is a subtle vessel.
Like a pillow recently slept on, it is warm
and soft. It beats, gently, a river

of life, like padded oars going out
on a dark sea, following some unforgivable mission.
Breath and blood are interchangeable,

like twins who always share clothing.
Yours is white, inviting colour
like cloth awaiting the natural dyes:

I carry one which is red. Descending
like a lover of flowers about to pick
a lily, fail to feel the prick of tongue

and fang, in the clouded delirium
of drainage. A moment we form one heart,
a single conduit of moveable force along

the path without resistance. Your murmurs
are much appreciated, they help overcome the sad loss
I afterwards consider, leaving the dry site of our kiss.

Bottles

Each poison is a different colour.
Glisten, sparkle, my liquid interlocutors.
Yellow for the spider-glass, spotted.
Black for the Atlantic, performed
in a rigid spill. White is vestal.

Dark green for the kiss of whores
betrayed by sailors, Cuchulainn's
sword dividing pears. Purple
is the ring prisoners wear
to the throne. Red's inside,

pondering. Red shocks, sly
evacuee. White seeps,
the hand examining gel
love parts through wild hair.
Yellow for the promise of dead bees

brought me in a basket, like new-
fallen apples, bright and crisp, senseless
unless bitten. Black is a mouth
dipped in the cellar, opening
red wine. Blue is unlikely

at night, yet apparent, often closer
to the moon than colour. Each
poison is a label I peel like an elaborate
grape, a game spun by a shipwreck,
to entangle answers, keep her by the bracelet.

For Pierina at Christmas

You have asked for something
simple, direct and full of meaning
to wrap around this season
like a bow: here is your string

of words, then, tied tight
against a box of air, empty
except for how it wants
to be perfect, for your opening

glance. A poem is present only
in how it fits the paper,
well and good, like a man
will hold a woman, for

an hour, without either one
of them bothering to remove
a hand, or give any thought
to clothing.

The Kite Flyer

knows she is in the wrong business
if escape is uppermost
in her mind: lengthens the curve

of string to tighten the wind, and drives
across winter from above, her bird
hunting after currents, folds

in sky affairs, strengthening
play and purpose in a mild force
of handiwork, the resourceful box swerving

to maintain the depth, and height
of the moon, the line. The blue
in air is rapid, achieved through steering

by sheer delight, and unbroken plans
urging spirits out of things, to mean
the motor and suspension wild in touch, her flight.

Mary Veronica Swift, 1914-1991

1

The cosmology of a room is uneven.
It has containment and leakage the heavens
cannot hold or set, it has been lived through,
beds the weight and blood of persons
having moved, and traced, their outlines
by breath and dying. Mary Veronica Swift,
you fell in passing from your comforter,
your head abruptly struck
where the white radiator's iron coiled.

2

I have brought away trinkets from where you died,
Christs bent into each conceivable trident of pain,
and will fit them to purposes on my Verdun wall.
Paint leaps at the hammer, cracked like ice
in the Arctic as it heaves, to both sides, broken.
Plaster flours my fingers, leavened hands
setting aside Mother and Child
to inspect the damage:
a Nile zigzags from baseboard to ceiling.

3

Now I hang your Dublin cross,
made of fine linen,
saved behind glass in a frame
no bigger than a face;
suffer no debt or anger
but the loss of love.
Wielding a substance known as light,
I rise to strike, like Hephaestus
tempering his blow
against the pagan nail.

Suburbia Mythologica

Put off that mask of burning gold —W.B.Yeats

    1

She would not take the mask off.
She waited, as if to be sacrificed:
had taken off her clothes
and was lying still,
even holding her stomach in
to suppress deep breath,
and let the light in
only through the thick jewellery
of the artificial eyes.
Her hands held broken glass,
she was content with this.

I gave her a kiss,
and let her sleep it off.
I held a coffee
in the den all night,
relaxed with my mercy
and my lack of sex.
In the morning I went off to work,
with dark marks
curved under my eyes.

    2

When I came home
up the path past the tricycle,
the son was poking the mask
to make it rock
with the long prod of a plastic rifle,
as if it were an overturned turtle
or cradle.

I looked into the hollow face-guard
where it fitted on, where the soft meat
of the turtle would be exposed.
We kicked the left-over, antique
head-vase from a sweatier,
more metallurgic age,
to the garbage can,
dropped it in like a virgin
down a volcano,
and lidded it with tin.

The next morning
on my way to work
two men jumped off
the back of a truck
like the unemployed
from a train, and heaved cans
like armoured bodies
into the grinding
cleaving visor,
and heard no more of the mask
than the sound of bronze
collapsing.

3

Now I want her every night,
as if something potent
has pricked into my heart
with the silent spurt of a blow-dart.
She is common Form become Ideal,
and does not consider me
enough to let me interfere
with her revolutions through the house,
celestially at calm,
her hands healing
under the bandages of an apron.

She says I have killed her son,
but I look in on him
and the moon of light
through the door
shows him tired out
like any living child,
breathing soft mushrooms
up through the blanket
over his nose and eyes.

She says she had another one,
puts her hands like jug handles
at her hips, to scold:
he was not in me,
he grew in the mask;
he was going to come out of the mouth,
the ancient, unreal half.

Then, she locks the bedroom
and leaves herself to cold heaven
in sleeping cream.

Ways of Counting

When next I see you see me,
You will be young, I will be thirty.

Years are like fans in plays by Oscar Wilde.
Ladies open them, part of the scenery.

In your hands shake out our days.
They beat the air, cool our faces.

Each fold, tinted variously, is a time,
And the beauty of the whole was planned.

Now I am alone, until rejoined,
When you decide to finish the book of us

Borrowed by a friend. It is body
And mind, mind and body, being so extended.

When next I feel you feel mine,
I will be like a fork given back its favourite tine.

Florence, South Carolina

Dante was not born here.
Still, there is some heat

intact in the air, laid on the ground,
circled by sun, preserved

beside the shuddering Greyhound.
We occupy, for now, a forlorn

terminal of halted outdoor clocks:
each rusted hand takes two hours

to circumnavigate the face. A black man
loiters in his brown suit, time-travelled

wrinkles scheme against the boring light.
One old woman, definitely spinster, white,

grimly, in her summer dress, looks
straight ahead, too proud to get on,

too poor to own any other option.
Our driver leans against his Marlboro,

the size of a king, fulfilling a kind of rest.
Dust pours and burns throughout

the impolitic bus, urinated with torpor.
Finally, beginning to linger back to our seats,

we passengers come to terms with our lot.
The motor rattles between death and life.

Motion and the motor become us all at once,
shunting us far from this deep, hot half-place.

I, holding onto a parcel, a girl's sweet-altered face.
She was this dismal station's small-town Beatrice.

To Spiders

They are excellent hosts
to faithful flies, lost
in their fragile rafters,
gods of a light church

in awe only of the broom, Raid,
cold trappists who travel out
to the close Mecca of their prey,
and, kneeling at the twisted bread,

knead blood with fingers thin as air,
to taste the sour writhing there,
bodies who come, without desire,
to be dead. These creatures that look

comfortably cruel, miswritten
as the number 8, are spools of poison
coiled like frost magnets, masquerading
as insects but devoid

of even that humanity,
spreading their thin, cost-effective product
thick as love, before the orgy drains out
a sexless fate, its liquefying cost.

Life-defying feats are easy
for the thirst artist arachnid, risen
like yeast on a near-visible, stark trapeze.
They vandalise corpses in the husked breeze.

"Flight Delayed"

So says the board. And elsewhere
somebody knows something more.
But here we wait with flowers that

will never see vases, earnest arms
that won't be thrown around necks,
limo drivers that can just go home.

There are toys and voice recordings
in tropical water and dresses in trees.
We continue standing before words

so discreet as to be plainly insulting
to what is about to become obscene
time. There could be another reason,

many meanings we might tolerate.
Stacked-up, de-icing, cross-winds.
Phones full, it's a hospital waiting

to happen, husbands pacing like a birth
were in the air. Wives walk shy circles.
As other arrivals and departures appear,

living's ordinary irony, a bare normalcy,
makes everything else now tight and dull.
Soon we will travel to a big careful room

with a hundred others and break
while a very polite spokesperson
tries to explain the rest of our life.

I want all her luggage back, want to see it
yanked from the carousel by her own hand.
The good coffee is black and hot and sweet.

The world is come down to filling forms.
We are like students sitting a hard exam.
I lean over to see another man's answers.

He has written a short name in every box.
On each line, the same. Several time zones
away there are uniforms lifting in the dawn.

Of Adonis I Sing, and Aphrodite

Adonis is not with us.
He nurses
a thigh hit by a boar,

the infinite attraction
of what can't be had
his current location

in the always hard
to find Hades. Wanting
is getting for a goddess,

Death is fame gone mad,
glamorous, sexy, enigmatic.
Life is static, compared

to where Adonis waits
for beautiful love
to buy him out

for wild nights,
the poster boy
of the perfect chest, thighs

and erection, hunting
between her legs
for a trophy

he could have in any glade
from any maiden. Bored,
he left her, wanting more.

Who wants to be him
or her, when there is Hades
itself, warm as the anus

of Achilles or Tranus,
always the best origin
to return to, if chased

by a *femme* immortal?
Ah, Aphrodite, do not be sad.
In Hades, Adonis can be had

if truth be poetry
and the lyric told.
Go, and be Latinate

on your bitter date.
Or stay, and praise
the sun's old rays.

Either is satisfying,
and not like dying.
In Hades they come together,

like a bird losing a feather
to gain a wing.
So, of all lovers let us sing.

To adore is best where
man, woman and beast
commingle, on the spine

of pleasure, the utter
erotic tingle, as orifice,
and Orpheus, intertwine.

Eros Victorious

The white throat thrown back muscular
and smooth, its own animal in transition
from power to restraint, an ocean still
skin which another Aeneas slides upon,

devouring the ancestral nationalities of
ghostly blood that swims under it all,
love and the bowl speaking a discovery
of a living mouth pulsing saliva, sweet

harboring of thought and meat, jointed
where both worlds gate out. Marble
sinews through the hours of cast sight,
shadowing the silver eye no god opens,

and music undulant and within, spills
a glass finger of excessive light, hard
and softest things salt and fresh, fast
as the river and body involve tongues.

No war, no enmity, no towers hold,
peace in the struck, wet encampment
tenting the standards and the soldiery,
the slack chargers, broad necks bowed,

each gold arrow in its tight quiver,
shields sleeping bronze in night cold,
and hot generals bent over the throne
taking on themselves a defeated lash,

as ash stands attentive in the vase,
all wax and incense laid to waste,
smoke like a moan in sudden air,
where maid and mortal boil away

the water of their passion to a misted heat.
Their bed is the capital that has been won,
as every history must be rewritten now,
to tell vanquished and victorious apart.

Aerial Bombardment, Serbia, Spring 1999

Hovering over the anvil, the hammer.
In the air, a phantom turns
and light creates destruction below.

Always the something superimposed,
not yet there, for now unfallen:
the sword of Damocles (or NATO),

the penis of the hero, about to deflower,
the sleek silent weapon trembling
and Death as fine and golden as a hair.

The pen before it touches down on paper.
A mouth so close it becomes the other mouth.
Your hand, aloft as if to swear a truth

or strike me for an infidel on my bowed head.
All balances on all, perpetual, close
contact postponed, an arrow in trajectory, until:

a word ballistic, a subtle act, made catastrophe.
Icing spread softly across the cake.
A body murdered of blood, an inch above her bed.

Gorazde

Men and women are small
when bullets are put inside them,
they lie down like stones.
All the bodies leaning on the ground.

Like children throwing glass at rain,
this could almost be strange new fun;
even when you are dead, gentlemen,
no one will forget what you have done.

Todd Swift was born on Good Friday in 1966, and grew up in St-Lambert and Montreal, Quebec. He is a freelance screenwriter for television and film, and has had work produced by Fox, Paramount and HBO. His feature film script (with Stanley Whyte), *Fugue State*, was recently optioned. Working as part of the performance duo Swifty Lazarus (with Tom Walsh), he has written the words for Jose Navas' acclaimed dance piece *Sterile Fields*, and appeared on the CD *Millennium Cabaret*, as well as on CBC radio. Swift's articles and poems have appeared in many publications, including *Prism International*, *Matrix*, *Quarry*, *Classic Forum*, *Himself* (Ireland), *Budapest Style* and *enRoute*. He has performed his poetry widely in North America and Europe. In 1998-99 he was Guest Lecturer at ELTE University in Budapest.